CARING FOR KEMP'S RIDLEY TURTLES

A SHORT GUIDE ON PET OWNERSHIP AND CARE

DR MORRIS HART

Copyright© 2024 **DR MORRIS HART**

Table of Contents

Introduction

Named after Richard Moore Kemp, who first described the species in 1880, Kemp's Ridley turtles, scientifically known as Lepidochelys kempii, are among the smallest and most critically endangered species of sea turtles in the world. Their distinct appearance and behavior have captured the hearts of turtle enthusiasts all over the world.

This in-depth guide will cover the natural history, habitat, physical attributes, behavior, and conservation status of Kemp's Ridley turtles, providing prospective owners with the knowledge they need to make an informed decision about keeping these amazing animals as pets.

Natural History

Native to the western Atlantic Ocean and the Gulf of Mexico, Kemp's Ridley turtles primarily nest along the coast of Tamaulipas, Mexico; they are also occasionally found in waters off the eastern coast of the United States, mainly in the Atlantic coast from Florida to North Carolina and the Gulf of Mexico.

Primarily carnivorous, these turtles consume a wide range of marine invertebrates, including crabs, jellyfish, shrimp, and mollusks. They are distinguished by their synchronized nesting behavior, which is unique among sea turtles and involves large groups of females coming ashore at the same time to lay their eggs at arribadas, or mass nesting events. This behavior is believed to offer protection against predators.

Physical attributes

The look of Kemp's Ridley turtles is characteristic and distinguishes them from other species of sea turtles.

Their carapace (shell) is oval in shape and varies in color from olive-green to grayish-brown. The underside of the shell is usually pale yellow or white.

The average adult Kemp's Ridley turtle weighs approximately 100 pounds (45 kilograms) and has a carapace length of 24 to 28 inches (61 to 71 centimeters). However, records show that some individuals have reached as high as 30 inches (76 centimeters) in length.

Actions

In addition to being highly migratory, Kemp's Ridley turtles are known for their social behavior, frequently congregating in groups in nearshore waters. During the nesting season, females travel hundreds or even thousands of miles to lay their eggs on the beaches where they were born.

Kemp's Ridley turtles are known for their coordinated nesting patterns, but they also engage in other fascinating activities like elaborate wooing displays during the mating season and sunbathing in the sun to control their body temperature.

Status of Conservation

Even though they are among the smallest species of sea turtles, Kemp's Ridleys are threatened on many fronts. In the past, their numbers were drastically reduced due to overexploitation of their meat, eggs, and shells. Currently, they are threatened by habitat loss, pollution, climate change, and accidental entrapment in fishing gear.

As a result, conservation efforts are being made to protect their nesting beaches, reduce bycatch in fishing gear, and raise public awareness about the importance of preserving their habitat. Kemp's Ridley turtles are protected by various laws and regulations and are classified as critically endangered by the International Union for Conservation of Nature (IUCN).

Kemp's Ridley turtles are amazing animals with a fascinating natural history and distinctive behavioral features. Although they have many difficulties in the wild, they can flourish in captivity with the right care from knowledgeable and committed owners. Pet owners can help to ensure the survival of this iconic species for future generations by being aware of their needs and respecting their conservation status.

Chapter 1

Selecting the Appropriate Setting for Kemp's Ridley Turtles

For the health and well-being of Kemp's Ridley turtles, it is imperative that they have an ideal environment. In this section, we will discuss the important aspects to take into account when designing a suitable habitat for these special reptiles, such as tank size, substrate, lighting, water quality, temperature, and enrichment.

Dimensions & Setup of the Tank

The first thing to think about when creating an environment for Kemp's Ridley turtles is the size and arrangement of their tank. These turtles need lots of room to swim, explore, and behave like turtles, so you should aim to provide them with at least 10 gallons of water for every inch of shell length.

Once they reach adulthood, Kemp's Ridley turtles may need larger tanks, ranging from 75 gallons to over 100 gallons, depending on their size and activity level. For juvenile turtles, a tank capacity of 40 to 75 gallons is acceptable, giving them opportunity to grow and develop.

When choosing a tank, think about its size and design. Round or tall tanks are less likely to have enough surface area for swimming and sunbathing than rectangular tanks. Make sure the tank has a tight-fitting top to keep the turtle safe.

Water Purity

Kemp's Ridley turtles depend on optimal water quality, which can only be achieved through routine filtration and water changes that eliminate waste and stop toxic and hazardous bacteria from growing.

Purchase a high-quality filtration system made especially for holding turtles, like a canister filter or a hybrid system that combines mechanical and biological filtration. Select a filter whose flow rate is suitable for the tank's capacity.

A pH of 6.5 to 7.5, a temperature range of 75 to 85°F (24 to 29°C), and ammonia and nitrite levels close to zero are the ideal water conditions for Kemp's Ridley turtles. Regularly check temperature, pH, ammonia, nitrite, and nitrate levels with test kits.

Establish a basking area with a UVB light to supply vital ultraviolet (UV) radiation for calcium metabolism and vitamin D production, and a heat lamp so the turtle can adjust its body temperature and dry off fully after swimming.

Substance

For optimal water quality and to support natural activities, the substrate used in a Kemp's Ridley turtle tank should be chosen carefully. Turtles may choke on gravel or small rocks, which can lead to stomach problems.

Large river boulders, smooth stones, or aquarium-safe sand are good substrate options since they are easy to clean and provide the turtle a realistic environment to explore. Just make sure to rinse the substrate well before adding it to the tank to get rid of any dust or dirt.

Decoration and Enhancement

Kemp's Ridley turtles require a variety of floating and submerged objects to interact with, such as driftwood, aquatic plants, PVC pipes, and floating platforms. Enrichment is a crucial component of creating a stimulating environment for these turtles.

In addition to adding visual interest to the tank, aquatic plants also provide the turtle with hiding places and areas to graze. Choose resilient, turtle-safe plants like Java fern, hornwort, and anubias that can tolerate nibbling and still give oxygenation.

Include hiding places and caves in the tank design to provide the turtle with a feeling of security and seclusion. These can be made from stacked rocks, ceramic caves, or prefabricated turtle hides; just make sure that everything is anchored firmly to keep decorations from falling over and hurting the turtle.

Regular maintenance and monitoring are essential to create a safe and thriving habitat for these amazing reptiles. Pet owners can ensure the health and well-being of their turtles for years to come by carefully considering the unique needs and behaviors of Kemp's Ridley turtles. This can be achieved by providing a spacious tank with clean water, appropriate substrate, and enriching décor.

Chapter 2

Guidelines for Nutrition and Feeding Kemp's Ridley Turtles

The health and well-being of Kemp's Ridley turtles depend on proper nutrition. In this extensive guide, we will examine the dietary needs, feeding practices, and nutrition guidelines specific to these unusual reptiles, including suggestions for juvenile and adult turtles.

nutritional requirements

In their natural habitat, Kemp's Ridley turtles consume a wide range of marine invertebrates, such as crabs, shrimp, jellyfish, mollusks, and other small prey items. Since they are carnivorous, it is important to mimic their natural diet as closely as possible in captivity to maintain optimal health and nutrition.

High-quality commercial turtle pellets or sticks made especially for aquatic turtles can be a staple food source for Kemp's Ridleys. Look for products that contain a combination of animal proteins, like fish meal, shrimp meal, and insect meal, as well as necessary vitamins and minerals. A balanced diet for Kemp's Ridleys should include a variety of protein sources, vitamins, and minerals.

To supplement commercial turtle pellets and encourage natural hunting behaviors, provide a variety of live or frozen prey items, such as earthworms, mealworms, crickets, brine shrimp, and bloodworms, in addition to live or frozen feeder fish.

Feeding Patterns

In the wild, Kemp's Ridley turtles seek for food along the seafloor and in shallow coastal waters, using their powerful jaws to crush and ingest animals. These turtles are opportunistic feeders, meaning they will eat food whenever it is available.

Offering food items in tiny quantities to prevent overfeeding and keeping an eye on the turtle's bodily condition to make sure it is maintaining a healthy weight are two enjoyable aspects of caring for Kemp's Ridley turtles in captivity.

Adult turtles can be fed every other day to avoid obesity and to maintain ideal health; juvenile turtles can be fed daily to meet their nutritional needs during the rapid growth phase, with a combination of commercial pellets and live or frozen prey items.

It's critical to monitor feeding behavior and modify the diet in accordance with the turtle's dietary needs and preferences. Certain turtles may have specific dietary preferences, and others may need vitamin and mineral supplements to maintain a balanced diet.

Supplements for Nutrition

To make sure they are getting all the vitamins and minerals they need, Kemp's Ridley turtles may benefit from sporadic nutritional supplements in addition to a diversified diet of commercial pellets and live or frozen prey items.

For the development of a turtle's shell, calcium and vitamin D3 are especially important. Before feeding live prey items to the turtle, dust them with a calcium supplement powder that contains vitamin D3. Alternatively, provide the turtle with a calcium supplement in the form of a cuttlebone or calcium block to gnaw on as needed.

Additionally, Kemp's Ridley turtles who are not receiving a varied diet may benefit from multivitamin supplements; select a multivitamin supplement designed specifically for reptiles and adhere to the recommended dosage and frequency of administration.

Hydration and Water

Kemp's Ridley turtles get most of their water from their diet and surroundings, so it's important to keep them properly hydrated. Make sure fresh, clean water is always available for swimming and drinking.

In order to prevent dehydration, provide a shallow water dish or tray in the enclosure for the turtle to sip from and soak in. Be sure to periodically check the water level and replenish the dish as needed.

The nutrition and feeding of Kemp's Ridley turtles are vital to their health and well-being. Pet owners can guarantee that their turtles receive the necessary nutrients for a healthy life in captivity by offering a balanced diet of commercial pellets, live or frozen prey, and nutritional supplements as needed. Responsible turtle care also includes behavior observation, feeding habits monitoring, and diet adjustments. Kemp's Ridley turtles can live long, healthy lives in captivity with proper nutrition and attention to dietary requirements.

Chapter 3

Some Wellness and Health Advice for Kemp's Ridley Turtles

Kemp's Ridley turtle longevity and quality of life depend on maintaining their health and well-being. In this extensive guide, we will cover a wide range of topics related to turtle health, such as common ailments, preventative care, environmental influences, and veterinary care considerations.

Typical Health Concerns

Both in the wild and in captivity, Kemp's Ridley turtles are vulnerable to a wide range of health disorders. Keeping these unusual reptiles healthy requires knowledge of these concerns and proactive steps to avoid and treat them.

Shell Rot: Usually brought on by dirty water or insufficient sun exposure, shell rot is a common bacterial infection that causes lesions, foul-smelling lesions, and softening or discoloration of the turtle's shell. It can be treated quickly with topical antibiotics and requires better husbandry techniques.

Kemp's Ridley turtles may develop respiratory infections as a result of low-quality water, insufficient basking temperatures, or exposure to drafts. These infections can manifest as wheezing, gasping for air, nasal discharge, and lethargy. Treatment for respiratory infections usually consists of supportive care combined with antibiotics to minimize symptoms and avoid complications.

Metabolic Bone Disease (MBD): Treatment for MBD in turtles involves supplementing with calcium and vitamin D3, as well as making dietary and husbandry changes to prevent recurrence. MBD is a common nutritional disorder caused by calcium and vitamin D3 deficiencies. Symptoms include softening of the shell, swollen joints, lethargy, and difficulty moving.

Treatment for parasitic infections in Kemp's Ridley turtles includes antiparasitic medications prescribed by a veterinarian. External parasites that can affect the turtles include nematodes, protozoa, and ectoparasites like ticks and mites. Symptoms of parasitic infections vary depending on the type of parasite but may include diarrhea, weight loss, lethargy, and skin lesions.

Preventive Healthcare Practices

Maintaining the health and well-being of Kemp's Ridley turtles and reducing the likelihood of health concerns require preventive care. The following actions can help avert frequent diseases and enhance general wellbeing:

Maintain Clean Water: Kemp's Ridley turtles require clean, healthy water, which can only be achieved through routine water changes and filtration. Water quality criteria including temperature, pH, ammonia, nitrite, and nitrate levels should be constantly monitored, and corrective action should be taken as necessary.

Provide Enough Opportunities for Basking: Kemp's Ridley turtles need access to a space big enough for them to stretch their limbs fully and under a UVB lamp, which will provide them with the necessary UV radiation for vitamin D synthesis. The space should also have a heat lamp so the turtles can regulate their body temperature and dry off completely after swimming.

Offer a Balanced Diet: To guarantee that Kemp's Ridley turtles receive all the nutrients they need, offer a varied diet that includes commercial turtle pellets, live or frozen prey, and sporadic nutritional supplements. Keep an eye on feeding habits and make necessary diet adjustments based on the turtle's preferences and nutritional needs.

Maintain Appropriate Humidity Levels: To avoid dehydration and to keep their skin and shell in good condition, Kemp's Ridley turtles need a humid environment. Keep an eye on the humidity levels in the turtle's enclosure and provide more moisture as needed by misting it frequently or using a humidifier.

Seek veterinary assistance as soon as you discover any abnormalities or concerns regarding the turtle's health. Keep an eye out for Behavioral Changes: Keep an eye out for changes in the turtle's behavior, hunger, and activity level since these can be early indicators of health problems.

Environmental Elements

The health and happiness of Kemp's Ridley turtles are greatly influenced by environmental factors. To guarantee the best possible health and happiness, a suitable habitat that satisfies the turtles' unique demands and preferences must be created.

Temperature: To replicate the circumstances of their natural habitat, keep the water at 75 to 85°F (24 to 29°C) and the basking area at 85 to 90°F (29 to 32°C). Kemp's Ridley turtles are ectothermic reptiles, meaning they depend on outside heat sources to control their body temperature.

Lighting: To mimic natural sunshine and encourage the synthesis of vitamin D3 in Kemp's Ridley turtles, use a UVB lamp with a wavelength of 290 to 320 nanometers. Place the UVB lamp over the basking area and change the bulb every six to twelve months to guarantee optimal performance.

Habitat Enrichment: Incorporate aquatic plants, rocks, driftwood, and PVC pipes into the tank design to create a diverse and interesting habitat for the turtle to explore. Decorate the turtle's habitat with a variety of substrates, hiding places, and decorations to promote natural behaviors and mental stimulation.

Considerations for Veterinary Care

Selecting a veterinarian with experience and skill in reptile medicine is vital when choosing a physician for your turtle. Regular veterinary treatment is necessary for monitoring the health and wellness of Kemp's Ridley turtles and resolving any underlying health issues or concerns.

Plan yearly wellness exams with a reptile veterinarian to evaluate the turtle's overall health, conduct diagnostic tests, and talk about preventive care. The veterinarian will examine the turtle's body condition, shell condition, and behavior during the exam, and if necessary, they may suggest further testing or treatments.

Along with routine examinations, if you notice any changes in the turtle's appetite, lethargy, abnormal behavior, or physical abnormalities, get in touch with a veterinarian right away. Early detection and intervention can help prevent complications and improve the course of treatment.

Kemp's Ridley turtles have unique needs and preferences, so it's important to pay close attention to those. Pet owners can make sure their turtles live long, healthy lives in captivity by putting preventive care measures in place, keeping an eye on environmental factors, and seeking veterinary care when necessary. With the right care and attention, Kemp's Ridley turtles can thrive and bring joy to their owners for many years to come.

Chapter 4

Activities for Enrichment and Interaction with Kemp's Ridley Turtles

In this thorough guide, we will cover several activities and enrichment tactics to keep these unique reptiles interested, active, and healthy in captivity. Providing chances for contact and enrichment is crucial for the physical and mental well-being of Kemp's Ridley turtles.

Comprehending the Behavior of Turtles

Kemp's Ridley turtles are curious, energetic reptiles that spend much of their time swimming, hunting for food, and sunbathing. It's crucial to understand their behaviors and preferences before plunging into interaction and enrichment activities.

Kemp's Ridley turtles in captivity gain from having the chance to explore their surroundings and participate in these natural behaviors; pet owners can encourage physical activity, mental stimulation, and general well-being by offering enrichment activities that replicate their natural habitat and pique their senses.

Exercise and Swimming

The first step in encouraging swimming and exercise for Kemp's Ridley turtles is to provide a large tank with clean, warm water. Swimming is a crucial activity for these turtles, as it allows them to maintain cardiovascular health, exercise their muscles, and explore their environment.

Incorporate floating objects like basking platforms, logs, and aquatic plants to provide resting sites and encourage exploration. To promote swimming, design a tank layout with open swimming regions, hiding places, caverns, and obstacles for the turtle to maneuver around.

A variety of enrichment items, changed occasionally to keep the turtle occupied and prevent boredom, should be provided; regularly observe the turtle's swimming behavior and adapt the tank layout to suit their preferences and activity level.

Enhancement of Food and Foraging

In captivity, offering opportunities for foraging and food enrichment can engage the senses and enhance brain stimulation in Kemp's Ridley turtles, which forage for food along the seafloor and in shallow coastal waters as part of their natural behavior.

Dispersing food items throughout the tank or hiding them inside enrichment items like floating balls, puzzle feeders, or PVC tubes are some ways to integrate foraging into the turtle's daily routine. This encourages the turtle to actively search for and retrieve its food, simulating the difficulties of foraging in the wild.

To keep the turtle interested and avoid habituation, rotate the food enrichment items on a regular basis. Vary the textures, shapes, and sizes of the food items to provide the turtle variation and to excite its senses.

Bathing and Exposure to Sunlight

Offering a suitable basking area with access to UVB lighting is essential for the health and well-being of Kemp's Ridley turtles, as basking allows them to regulate their body temperature, dry off completely after swimming, and absorb essential ultraviolet (UV) radiation for vitamin D synthesis.

It is Certain that the basking area is sufficiently large to allow the turtle to completely extend its limbs and that it is situated beneath a UVB lamp with a wavelength of 290 to 320 nanometers. Consistently observe the turtle's basking behavior and make necessary adjustments to the UVB lamp's position and intensity to maintain optimal exposure.

Position the basking area close to the water's surface so that the turtle may easily move from swimming to sunbathing. Add more enrichment materials, such as plants, driftwood, and rocks, to the basking area to create a naturalistic and welcoming habitat for the turtle.

Enhancement of Environment

The term "environmental enrichment" refers to a range of activities and stimuli that are intended to support natural behaviors, mental stimulation, and the general well-being of Kemp's Ridley turtles. The following enrichment tactics can be implemented in the turtle's surroundings:

- Give the turtle a range of surfaces, textures, and substrates to investigate, such as sand, smooth rocks, and water plants.

- To keep the habitat interesting and avoid habituation, rotate and reorganize enrichment items, hiding places, and tank decorations on a regular basis.

- Provide the turtle with new objects to explore and play with, such as mirrors and floating toys.

- To create a tranquil environment for the turtle, play soft, relaxing music or natural noises.

- Provide the turtle with grazing areas, hiding places, and visual appeal by adding real or artificial greenery.

Social Communication

Even though Kemp's Ridley turtles are not gregarious creatures by nature, they might nevertheless gain from the occasional social interaction with their human caretakers. Visiting the turtle in its tank, chatting with it, and providing it with tender caresses or handling can all contribute to the development of trust and bolster the relationship between the owner and their pet.

To prevent generating stress or anxiety, approach the turtle quietly and slowly when engaging in interaction.

Pay attention to the turtle's body language and behavior to see if it appears uncomfortable, and respect its limits if it becomes agitated or withdraws inside its shell.

To prevent overstimulation and minimize stress for the turtle, keep handling and interaction brief. To prevent injury or distress, never pick up the turtle by its limbs or shell; instead, support the turtle's body with both hands and allow it to move freely.

The promotion of Kemp's Ridley turtles' health, happiness, and well-being in captivity is largely dependent on interaction and enrichment activities. Pet owners can create an environment that is both stimulating and enriching for their turtles by offering opportunities for swimming, foraging, basking, and exploring. Frequent monitoring, observation, and adjustments to the turtle's environment and enrichment activities are necessary to ensure a rewarding and fulfilling experience for both the turtle and its owner.

Chapter 5

Legal Aspects and Conservation Activities Concerning Kemp's Ridley Turtles

The Kemp's Ridley turtle is a critically endangered species that faces several challenges to its survival. In this extensive guide, we will discuss the legislative protections that these turtles enjoy as well as the current conservation efforts that are being made to maintain their habitats and numbers.

Legal Defenses

To address threats like habitat loss, pollution, illegal trade, and accidental capture in fishing gear, Kemp's Ridley turtles are protected by a number of international, national, and regional laws and regulations aimed at halting their decline and fostering their recovery.

International Protections: Signatory to international conservation agreements like the Convention on International Trade in Endangered Species of Wild Fauna and Flora (CITES), countries are required to regulate and monitor the trade of Kemp's Ridley turtles and their products to prevent exploitation and ensure their conservation. Kemp's Ridley turtles are listed as critically endangered by the International Union for Conservation of Nature (IUCN) Red List of Threatened Species, which highlights their precarious conservation status on a global scale.

National Protections: The Endangered Species Act (ESA) of 1973, which forbids the harassment, capture, killing, or trade of endangered species and their habitats, protects Kemp's Ridley turtles in the United States. The

ESA establishes critical habitat areas and calls for the creation of recovery plans to bring populations back to sustainable levels.

Regional Protections: State and local laws and regulations protect Kemp's Ridley turtle nesting beaches and foraging areas along the Gulf of Mexico coast. These include prohibitions on development along the shore, lighting near the beach, and recreational activities that could disturb the turtles or their hatchlings.

Preservation Activities

A combination of research, monitoring, habitat restoration, public education, and outreach initiatives are used in conservation efforts to protect Kemp's Ridley turtles and their habitats. Government agencies, non-profit organizations, research institutions, and community stakeholders collaborate to address the complex challenges that these turtles face.

Conservation organizations like the National Park Service, U.S. Fish and Wildlife Service, and local non-profits work to identify and secure nesting sites, implement nest monitoring programs, and conduct research on nesting behavior and habitat preferences. Nesting beach conservation is a priority for Kemp's Ridley turtle conservation efforts.

Reducing Bycatch: Kemp's Ridley turtles are at great risk from accidental capture in fishing gear, or "bycatch," especially in commercial fisheries that operate in their foraging areas. Conservation efforts seek to reduce bycatch by developing and implementing turtle excluder devices (TEDs) and other modifications to gear that allow turtles to escape from fishing gear without being harmed.

The survival of Kemp's Ridley turtles and other marine species depends on the restoration and protection of critical habitats, such as seagrass beds, mangrove forests, and coastal wetlands. Projects aimed at restoring habitats include eradicating invasive species, reforesting areas with native plants, and lessening the effects of pollution and coastal development.

Research and Monitoring: To better understand Kemp's Ridley turtle ecology and guide conservation planning, scientific research and monitoring are essential components of conservation strategies and management decisions. Research projects concentrate on behavior, population dynamics, migration patterns, genetics, and health of the turtles.

Public Education and Outreach: Conservation organizations and government agencies work with local communities, schools, businesses, and stakeholders to promote responsible behavior, encourage stewardship of natural resources, and foster a culture of conservation. Public education and outreach initiatives are crucial for bringing attention to the predicament of Kemp's Ridley turtles and spurring action to protect them.

Volunteer Opportunities: Through beach monitoring, nest protection, habitat restoration, and public outreach programs, volunteer programs allow individuals to directly support Kemp's Ridley turtle conservation efforts. Volunteers are essential to supporting ongoing research and conservation initiatives and creating a network of committed advocates for turtle conservation.

We can ensure that Kemp's Ridley turtles continue to thrive for generations to come by implementing legal protections, supporting conservation initiatives, and raising awareness about the importance of preserving their habitats. Through ongoing research, monitoring, and collaboration, we can work together to safeguard these iconic marine reptiles and their ecosystems for the benefit of all. Kemp's Ridley turtle protection and conservation requires concerted efforts at the local, national, and international levels to address the complex threats facing these endangered species.

Chapter 6

FAQs Concerning the Care and Maintenance of Kemp's Ridley Turtle Pets

Can pets be maintained as Kemp's Ridley turtles?

It is true that Kemp's Ridley turtles can be kept as pets, but in order to give them the right care and habitat, one must be aware of their unique demands.

- Do Kemp's Ridley turtles face extinction?

It is true that Kemp's Ridley turtles are critically endangered. A number of factors, like pollution, habitat degradation, unintentional entrapment in fishing gear, and illicit trading, pose a threat to the turtles' survival.

- What size tank is necessary for Kemp's Ridley turtles?

Kemp's Ridley juveniles need tanks that hold between 40 and 75 gallons, but adult turtles may require larger tanks that hold up to 100 gallons, contingent upon their size and degree of activity.

- What foods do Kemp's Ridley turtles consume?

Primarily carnivorous, Kemp's Ridley turtles consume a range of marine invertebrates, including mollusks, shrimp, crabs, and jellyfish. They can be given commercial turtle pellets, frozen or live food, and sometimes nutritional supplements while kept in captivity.

- Do Kemp's Ridley sea turtles require a place to bask?

Yes, a heat lamp-equipped basking area is necessary for Kemp's Ridley turtles to maintain their body temperature and dry off fully after swimming. A UVB lamp should be installed in the basking area as well to supply the necessary UV radiation for the production of vitamin D.

- How frequently should turtles named Kemp's Ridley be fed?

To avoid obesity and preserve good health, adult Kemp's Ridley turtles should only be fed every other day. Juvenile turtles can be fed everyday. Provide a diversified diet of commercial turtle pellets, frozen or live prey, and sporadic dietary supplements.

- What is the required water temperature for Kemp's Ridley turtles?

Kemp's Ridley turtles need water that is between 75 and 85°F (24 and 29°C) in order to stay healthy and happy. To keep the water temperature within this range, choose an aquarium heater that is dependable.

- Are animals with Kemp's Ridley turtles social?

Although Kemp's Ridley turtles are not gregarious creatures by nature, they might nevertheless gain from the occasional chance to socialize with their human caretakers. To prevent producing stress or worry, handle the turtle and engage with it in a calm and gradual manner.

- Is it permissible to keep Kemp's Ridley turtles as pets?

Legal limitations and rules may apply to the possession of Kemp's Ridley turtles as pets in some areas. Before obtaining a Kemp's Ridley turtle as a pet, it is imperative to investigate local laws and regulations surrounding the ownership and possession of endangered species.

- What is the lifespan of Kemp's Ridley turtles?

In captivity, Kemp's Ridley turtles can live up to 50 years or longer if given the right care and environment. Kemp's Ridley turtles can have long, robust lives in captivity with proper diet, medical attention, and environmental enrichment.

Recall that caring for a Kemp's Ridley turtle involves time, effort, expertise, and money in order to guarantee the health and welfare of these threatened species. Before getting a Kemp's Ridley turtle as a pet, think through the duties carefully and get advice from knowledgeable reptile keepers or turtle care specialists.

Chapter 7

Wrap-Up: Take Care of Your Kemp's Ridley Turtle and Have Fun

Although having a Kemp's Ridley turtle as a pet can be enjoyable, there are a lot of duties involved. In this last section, we will stress the value of responsible ownership and offer advice on how to take good care of and enjoy your Kemp's Ridley turtle while supporting its conservation and general health.

Conscientious Ownership

Understanding the unique needs and requirements of Kemp's Ridley turtles and giving them the right care, food, and habitat are the first steps in responsible ownership. It is our duty as guardians of these threatened species to make sure they flourish in captivity and support efforts to preserve them in the wild.

The following are essential guidelines for caring for Kemp's Ridley turtles responsibly:

Research and Education: Become knowledgeable about Kemp's Ridley turtles, including their natural history, habitat needs, and state of conservation. Keep up with the most recent advancements in turtle husbandry and seek advice on appropriate husbandry techniques from reliable sources.

Proper Habitat: To encourage natural behaviors and mental stimulation, provide a large tank with clean water, sufficient filtration, UVB lighting, a basking place, and enrichment items.

Nutritious Diet: To make sure your turtle gets all the nutrients it needs to be healthy, provide a varied diet that includes commercial turtle pellets, live or frozen prey, and occasionally nutritional supplements.

Regular Veterinary Care: Make an appointment for a wellness exam with a veterinarian that specializes in reptiles once a year to keep an eye on the turtle's health, address any issues or concerns, and get advice on preventive care.

Environmental Enrichment: To encourage movement, mental stimulation, and general wellbeing, include enrichment activities and stimuli in the turtle's surroundings.

Legal Compliance: Make sure you get your Kemp's Ridley turtle from reliable vendors who uphold the law and ethical standards. You should also obey any local rules and ordinances pertaining to the ownership and possession of these turtles.

Conservation Advocacy: By volunteering, donating to conservation organizations, and advocating for laws that support conservation, you may help save Kemp's Ridley turtles and their ecosystems.

Savoring Your Ridley Turtle

While proper ownership is crucial, Kemp's Ridley turtles have distinctive traits and behaviors that should be enjoyed and valued. For their owners, these amazing animals can offer countless hours of amusement, company, and wonder.

The following advice will help you and your Kemp's Ridley turtle get along and have fun:

Observation: Pay close attention to the interactions, behavior, and movements of your turtle. Discovering your turtle's unique personality and preferences can strengthen your relationship with it and help you better understand its requirements.

Regularly engage in interactions with your turtle by giving it gentle handling, feeding, and engaging in enrichment activities. Provide opportunities for swimming and basking, rearrange tank décor, and provide food enrichment items to encourage natural behaviors in your turtle. These are some examples of activities that will engage its senses.

Bonding Time: To build trust and reinforce your relationship, schedule specific time each day to spend with your turtle. As you converse and gently pet or scratch your turtle, pay attention to how it reacts to your presence. Use a soothing voice.

Enrichment Activities: To keep your turtle interested and entertained, come up with inventive enrichment activities and stimulation. Try a variety of enrichment objects, surfaces, and textures to pique the turtle's curiosity and encourage movement and exploration.

Learning Opportunities: Share what you've learned about these endangered animals and the significance of their protection with others by using your encounters with Kemp's Ridley turtles. To spread awareness and spur action, impart your knowledge and life experiences to friends, family, and neighbors.

Documentation: Take pictures, record movies, and keep a journal to track your turtle's development and achievements. Make a scrapbook or digital album to record the unique times and experiences you have with your turtle.

Community Involvement: Through online forums, social media groups, and regional reptile organizations, get in touch with other owners, aficionados, and conservationists of Kemp's Ridley turtles. With other turtle aficionados, exchange tales, pointers, and counsel to foster an informed and encouraging community.

Having a Kemp's Ridley turtle as a pet is an honor and a duty that calls for commitment, understanding, and kindness. You may have a happy and satisfying connection with these amazing animals by giving them the right care, food, and enrichment while also supporting their health, well-being, and conservation.

Always put your turtle's wellbeing first and take responsibility for their conservation and well-being as a steward. Kemp's Ridley turtles can flourish in captivity and help to ensure the survival of their species for future generations if given the right care and attention.

Take pleasure in the experience of nurturing and developing a relationship with your Kemp's Ridley turtle, and acknowledge the difference you're making in their life and the survival of their kind.

www.ingramcontent.com/pod-product-compliance
Lightning Source LLC
Chambersburg PA
CBHW051850250726
48659CB00006B/2128